Remarkable Names

of Real People

or

How to Name Your Baby

Hugh Pugh, Landscape Architect, London

Remarkable Names
of Real People

or

How to Name Your Baby

Compiled & annotated by
John Train

Illustrations by Pierre Le-Tan
Introduction by S. J. Perelman

Clarkson N. Potter, Inc., Publishers, New York
Distributed by Crown Publishers, Inc.

The portraits in this book are drawn entirely from my imagination and are in no way intended to be considered as likenesses or caricatures of the people named.

—Pierre Le-Tan

Published simultaneously in Canada by General Publishing Company Limited
First edition
Printed in the United States of America

Designed by Katy Homans
Type set in Monotype Dante by Michael & Winifred Bixler

Library of Congress Cataloging in Publication Data

Train, John.
  Remarkable names of real people.

  A new and expanded ed. of a booklet published privately in 1972 under title: How to name your baby.
  1. Names, Personal—Anecdotes, facetiae, satire, etc. I. Title.
CS2309.T72 1977   929.4   77-22058
ISBN 0-517-53130-5
Second Printing, December, 1977

Acknowledgments

The Office of Nomenclature Stabilization is grateful to its many faithful correspondents in the United States and abroad, starting with Joseph Fox, our collaborator for many years. Others are Timothy Dickinson, Margaret Bishop, her cousin Charles Harding and her brother Judge Don Young, George Plimpton, Candida Donadio, Robert Myrhum, Jennifer Raper, Frances Fosburgh, Peter Matthiessen, Nina Georges-Picot, S. J. Perelman, Brendan Gill, Alan Pryce-Jones, Jack Baumgarten, Howard Irwin, Clement Wood, Shelby Cullom Davis, Jerry Goodman, Pembroke Hart, Ormonde de Kay, Peter Thacher, Francine Lefrak, Robert Haynes, Fayette Hickox, Piers Dixon, Axie Whitney, Christopher Mallaby, Mrs. Doyle Klyn, Patricia Polak, Granya Gurevich, Kay Leperq, Richard Lamb, Leroy Morgan, Charles Chatfield, Joy Dineen, and Professors William Grierson, Howard Mumford Jones, Richard Gregg, Leonard Ashley, and Michael Coe. To the many whose diligence has not yet resulted in a verified entry, persevere! Those seriously interested in names should examine Percy H. Reaney's remarkable Origin of English Surnames, quod vide. *The Pliny of American onomastics was the indefatigable H. L. Mencken, to whom this little work is respectfully dedicated.*

Concerto Macaroni

PREFACE

Earlier this year, soon after the Indian electorate swept Indira Gandhi into the dustbin, a lady novelist named Lois Gould wrote a purportedly satiric piece for the New York Times. *Evidently her ire had been aroused by the statement of Morarji Desai, the new prime minister: "When a woman becomes devilish, she beats all the records. Now I can't say that she [Mrs. Gandhi] is all devil . . . but the good is suppressed and the devil is on top." Infuriated that Desai had thus kicked feminism in the groin, Miss Gould seized on comedy as an effective weapon to demolish him, and she conjectured three personalities for her lampoon—Dr. J. S. Mindblow of Harvard, Dr. R. V. Doppelgang of Yale, and a Dr. Tatiana Moxie, academic connection unspecified. The second I read these names, the* Times *fell from my nerveless hand and I was overcome by the mixture of neuralgia and depression that parlor comedians always induce in their auditors. That the fair columnist was as funny as a cry on the moors was instantly apparent, but I forced myself to finish her piece, and my suspicion was corroborated. As a novelist Miss Gould is doubtless superlative; I have yet to find out. As a wag, she had waded beyond her depth.*

What bearing, you may properly ask, has the foregoing on the present work? The answer is that try as it will, Art can never hope to surpass reality, and in assembling

7

this gallimaufry of actual names, the industrious Mr. Train has ransacked Nature to confirm the extraordinary riches of the world around us.

The people listed herein, let it be emphasized, are not fictional characters laboriously devised by the sophomoric to tickle the funny bone. They are real individuals, afflicted like the rest of us with bunions, flatulence, and presbyopia; folk who consult daily horoscopes, shlep their wetwash to the laundromat, fret about their sagging busts or their potency, and survive—God knows how—under the burden their parents have laid on them at the baptismal font. And because they do exist, they excite a dual response in the reader—an astonishment so vast that he dissolves into laughter, coupled with relief that his own name is pedestrian. That is, unless he is an Armenian named Pedestrian, in which case his gratification subsides like a toy balloon.

Along with the bizarrerie in these pages, however, it is worthy of note that very many of the names included have a distinct poetic or lyrical rhythm, and I can well imagine chanting oneself to sleep by repeating Sugarporn Poopatanna and Sistine Madonna McClung. I note with regret that the chronicler has seen fit to omit a heroine of my youth, Ming Toy Epstein, whose name had the sweet, tinkling purity of temple bells. He has, likewise, neglected to commemorate one Dolores del Schultz whom Dashiell Hammett once disclosed he met while a Pinkerton operative in San Francisco. As is inevitable in all works of scholarship, there are trifling minor errors; Toilet Jacobs was not a student at the Minneapolis School of Art but rather, as Lillian Hellman assured me, a schoolfellow of hers in New York.

8

Nonetheless, in culling such fragrant blooms from the files of newspapers, magazines, and educational institutions, Train and his network of informants have followed a great tradition. We know that Dickens' researches in the press and street directories of his day gave us immortalia like Dombey and Chuzzlewit, Podsnap, Uriah Heep, and Sairey Gamp—names resonant with authenticity, blessedly free of scamp-of-the-campus cuteness. Perhaps this collection will serve both as a reference work and a stimulus to others in the literary dodge to do the same.

—S. J. Perelman

Goody P. Creep, Undertaker

How to Name Your Baby

Too often well-intentioned parents, for lack of professional guidance, give their children names that stifle the infant's individuality. Psychologists remind us that an inappropriate name may affect a child's character: a dull name can mean a dull child. This guide is therefore offered to perplexed parents to suggest some possibilities they might not otherwise have considered. All of them are real names of real persons.

As most people know instinctively, there is a curious magic in names. If you call your little one Elmer *he is less likely to amount to anything than if you plunge in with a* Charlemagne *or a* Napoleon. *(Had the Emperor been christened* Gaston *he would surely have remained an obscure officer of artillery.)*

General Ulysses Grant . . . *what panache! Led by a* Hiram* *the boys in blue would have cracked; Gettysburg would have gone the other way. Under President* Oscar Lincoln *the Union would have been sundered. There would have been no Bicentennial.*

And speaking of panache, one knows that if Rostand had not celebrated Cyrano de Bergerac *but* Adolphe

---

*The General did in fact start life as Hiram.

Blanc *he would have flopped in the provinces and never made it to Paris, let alone to immortality.*

The Office of Nomenclature Stabilization was set up in the late 1940s to bring order to this situation. Over the years it has helped countless families on the verge of settling for Dora *or* Chick, *rose fanciers, racehorse breeders, yacht owners, and suburban home builders, and has sent many on their way rejoicing.*

To give an idea of the service, our favorite horticulturist is, quite properly, named Flor. *Excellent. But pretty girls will be wed. So the Office combed its files, alerted its correspondents, and has short-listed the following suitors:* Prof. della Flor, *botanist, author of* La Nostra Flora; Mr. Bloom, *horticulturist, Norfolk, Virginia;* Mr. Rose, *Head Gardener, Birmingham University School; and* Hyacinthe Ringrose, *attorney, New York City (among several dozen others). We understand that a selection is being made from these suitable names.*

In the following pages, then, anxious parents may see how others have solved the same problems they now confront. The examples, names of actual persons compiled over several decades, are arranged alphabetically by given name. One should look in the Index for one's family name, (e.g. Reuss, *on page 35) and then find the suggestions at the pages indicated.*

Every source cited (e.g. the New York Times) *is in our files and has been verified as carefully as time (and funds!) permit. Any corrections or later information will be gratefully received, together with nominations for the next edition—always, please, with documentation—ad-*

dressed to *The Office of Nomenclature Stabilization, 345 Park Avenue, New York, New York, 10022. Most undocumented submissions prove to be inaccurate or nonexistent. (Entries in the present text of whose authenticity we are satisfied but on which further information would be welcome are indicated thus: U.S.A.)*

Fifty years ago, contemplating Bible Belt folkways with fascinated dismay, H. L. Mencken* noted many prodigious given names, among which the following stand out: Chlorine, Coita, Dewdrop, Faucette, La Morte, Larceny, La Urine, Margorilla, Mecca, Merdina, Phalla, Twitty, Uretha, *and* Zippa *(female); and* Arson, Blasphemy, Blitzkrieg, Bugger, Cad, Constipation, *and* Overy *(male)*. Dinette *and* Lotowana *are in the 1933–34 New York* Social Register.

More recent candidates have come forward, however, whose claims are also hard to deny: Buzz Buzz *and* La Void†, *together with* Flourine Thermal *and—from Jamaica—*Little Tits.

From the large but, alas, unverified collection of Mr. George Hubbard of New York we find intriguing Aphrodite Chuckass, Heidi Yum-Yum Gluck, Sexious Boonjug, Sistine Madonna McClung *and* Zita Apathy. *We would welcome verification from our readers.*

---

*Supplement II: The American Language. *New York: Alfred A. Knopf, 1948.*

†*Peter Farb,* Word Play. *New York: Alfred A. Knopf, 1974.*

Mrs. Verbal Funderburk (*Lakeland, Florida*) *wrote to our collaborator, Professor William Grierson of the University of Florida, inquiring plaintively if she had the funniest name in the world. Fortunately, our earlier collection had just appeared. He sent his copy to her and her concern was laid to rest.*

Still in Florida, Mr. Everett Williams, Chief of the State's Bureau of Vital Statistics, has become overnight a figure of modest consequence in onomastic circles by releasing several discoveries, the result of many years' transactions of the Bureau, including Mac Aroni *and* Cigar Stubbs, *as well as* Teflon, Lavoris, *and* Truewillinglaughinglifebuckyboomermanifestdestiny *among given names. His position should permit Mr. Williams to perform an important role in the work of the Office, and we urge him on to redoubled efforts.*

As a by-product of détente we are considering an affiliate in the Soviet Union. After the Revolution, optimistic comrades favored names like Tractor *or* Electrification. *One enthusiast called his twin daughters* Anarchy *and* Utopia. *A frequent practice was to contrive such acronyms as* Melsor (*Marx-Engels-Lenin-Stalin-October-Revolution*).* *Now that the whole business has turned sour and become something one would rather not be reminded of, and with even* Pravda *deploring these "tasteless inventions," the classless parents are at a loss. Authoritative guidance*

*A Melsor *recently dropped the S (for Stalin) to become* Melor (Associated Press).

14

would, we understand, be welcome. We will be there. Our preliminary approved list includes Peaceful Coexistence *and* Virgin Lands *for girls, and for boys,* Norm, SAM, *and* Posthumus Rehabilitation.

Finally, the Office shares with its correspondents its satisfaction at the verification of Dr. Zoltan Ovary, on whom information was sought. Dr. Ovary proves to be a noted gynecologist, now at New York Hospital. Our respects to the Doctor, and, of course, to Madame Ovary.

J. T.

Aristotle Tottle, a very timid feeble pyrate

A. A. A. D'ARTAGNAN UMSLOPAGAAS
DYNAMITE MACAULAY
  (*London Times*)

A. MORON
  Commissioner of Education
  Virgin Islands

ANNE AASS
  Pittsburgh, Pennsylvania

APPENDICITIS, LARYNGITIS, MENINGITIS,
PERITONITIS, and TONSILLITIS JACKSON
  (*Newsweek*)

A. PRZYBYSZ*
  Detroit, Michigan

ARISTOTLE TOTTLE†
  Pirate
  Falmouth, England

Changed his name in 1940—to C. Przybysz. (Newsweek)

†*"A very timid, feeble Pyrate."* Gosse, A History of Piracy.

A. Toxen Worm
    Theatrical Press Agent
    New York City

Ave Maria Klinkenberg
    Yonkers, New York

Private Baby Cherry*
    U. S. Army
    (225th Quartermaster Battalion)

Bambina Broccoli†
    New York City

Basil Crapster‡
    Princeton University (Class of 1941)
    Princeton, New Jersey

*Compare Private Parts, U.S. Army, and Private Murder Smith, British Army.

†Compare Concerto Macaroni.

‡Compare E. C. Crapp, Washington, D. C.; Gladstone P. Lillycrap, U.S. Attorney; and Toilet Jacobs. Sharon Willfahrt and Tunis Wind were students of the Art Instruction School, Minneapolis, Minn.

SIR BASIL SMALLPEICE
    Chairman, Cunard Line
    London, England

BATHSHEBA FINKELSTEIN
    High School of Music & Art (Class of 1957)
    New York City

B. BROOKLYN BRIDGE
    (*John Hancock Life Insurance Company*)

REV. BLANCO WHITE*

BLUEY COLE SNOW
    (*John Hancock Life Insurance Company*)

MRS. BELCHER WACK WACK†

**A waverer. Ordained a priest in 1800; thereafter Professor
of Religion. Renounced Christianity and abandoned the
priesthood, 1810. Re-embraced Christianity, 1812; re-ordained,
1814.* (Dictionary of National Biography)

†*Miss Belcher married Mr. Wack and then married his
brother.*

BUGLESS, ENERGETIC, EUPHRATES, and
GOLIATH SMITH*
  (*Indexes of Births for England and Wales*)

MESSRS. BULL and SCHYTT
  Glaciologists
  General Assembly, International Union of
  Geodesy and Geophysics
  Geneva, Switzerland

BUNCHA LOVE†
  (*Newsweek*)

BUNYON SNIPES WOMBLE, Lawyer, and
CALDER WELLINGTON WOMBLE‡
  Winston-Salem, North Carolina

REVEREND CANAAN BANANA
  African National Council
  Rhodesia

*Cited in Dunkling, First Names First. London: J. M.
Dent and Sons, 1977*

†*Compare Felicity Pratt Love, Holy Love, and Wonderful
Love, all of New York. Miss Magnetic Love was a secretary in the
Army Air Corps. Hastie Love was convicted of rape in Tennessee.*

‡*"He enjoyed discussing the hyphen which in 1913 forever
linked the towns of Winston and Salem," and for which,
indeed, as head of the Winston Consolidation Committee, he was
in large measure responsible.*

Buncha Love

Cardinal Sin, Archbishop of Manila

Carborundum Petroleum Dobbs
   Mayor
   Wilmette, Illinois

Cardinal Sin
   Archbishop of Manila
   Philippines

Caresse Pecor
   University of Vermont (Class of 1971)
   Burlington, Vermont

Carlos Restrepo Restrepo Restrepo
de Restrepo
   Medellin, Colombia

Reverend Christian Church*
   Florence, Italy

Cigar Stubbs
   Florida
   Bureau of Vital Statistics

Col. Clarence Clapsaddle
   U. S. Army (West Point, Class of 1940)

---

*Active in 1966 flood relief effort. Compare Christ Apostle
and Conception de Jesus, both of New York City, and Rev. God,
of Congaree, S.C.*

SIR CLOUDSLEY SHOVEL*
Admiral, Royal Navy

MR. COCK MARRIED MISS PRICK†
(*London Times,* 1963)

CRAPPER, LIMITED, TOILETS‡
London, England

*Concluding a distinguished career, he ran the fleet on the
rocks (Scilly Isles) in 1707, drowning 2,000 men. After
struggling ashore, he was done in by a peasant woman who
"coveted an emerald ring on one of his fingers, and
extinguished his flickering life." He was buried in
Westminster Abbey, "where an elaborate monument in very
questionable taste was erected to his memory."* (Dictionary
of National Biography) *His gallant successor Admiral The
Hon. Sir Reginald Aylmer Ranfurley Plunkett-Ernle-Erle-Drax
participated in the Battle of Jutland. Captain Bigge Boozer
commanded the Guantanamo Naval Base, but Royal Naval
Shippe has opted for life ashore with the Federal Reserve
System, Washington, D.C.*

†*A Mr. Ora Jones married a Miss Ora Jones in 1941.*
(*R. L. Ripley*)

‡*Thomas Crapper's biography is aptly titled* Flushed With
Pride.

Sir Cloudesley Shovel, Admiral, Royal Navy

Cumming & Gooing, Louisiana

CUMMING & GOOING
Louisiana
(*New Yorker*)

DAPHNE READER'S DIGEST TAIONE
Utui, Vavao, Tonga

DEFRED GOO FOLTS
Director of Placement
Harvard Graduate School of Business
Administration
Cambridge, Massachusetts

DOCTOR DOCTOR*
(*American Medical Directory*)

*There were, by recent count, 13 doctors Doctor, Docter, or
Doktor in the U.S.; 5 doctors Bonebreak; 1 Bonecutter; 18
Butchers; several Cutters and Carvers; 184 Paines or Paynes
and 11 Pangs. Dr. Bonesetter practices in Bombay, and Dr.
Fillerup in Pasadena, Calif. as an obstetrician. Dr. Screech
practices in Victoria, British Columbia, and another Dr.
Screech is a dentist in Essex, England. For Dr. Ovary,
gynecologist, vide supra, p. 62. Among the Mormons, the
seventh son of a seventh son may be named Doctor. W.
Doctor Dollar, New York, has not yet entered the profession,
but should.*

D. Schumuk, Political Activist, Ukraine

D. Schumuk*
  Political Activist
  Ukraine, U. S. S. R.
  (*Reuters*)

Epaphroditus Marsh
Onesiphorus Marsh and
(Archbishop) Narcissus Marsh
  (*New York Times*)

Fanny Finger†
  New York City

*A loser. Served 7 years in jail (prewar) for communism.
Then (postwar) served 20 years and in 1972 started an
additional 10 years plus 5 years exile, all for anti-
communism.*

†*Compare Hyman Peckeroff, taxi driver, New York City;
and Hyman Pleasure, Assistant Commissioner, New York
State Department of Mental Hygiene.*

Charles Adolphe Faux-Pas Bidet*
    Commissaire de Police
    Paris, France

F. G. Vereneseneckockkrockoff†
    San Francisco, California

Firmin A. Gryp
    Banker
    Northern California Savings & Loan
    Association
    Palo Alto, California

(Madame) Fouqueau de Pussy‡
    Authoress

The Sûreté's ace on Russian intrigues, Faux-Pas Bidet received heavy press coverage in the 1930s when he investigated the abduction of Gen. Kutylpov, a White Russian leader in Paris. The general was seized in the street by OGPU agents and apparently, wrapped up as merchandise, was carried on board a Soviet ship, the Spartak, *which immediately put out to sea.*

†*Defendant in a celebrated murder trial in 1897. See* Jennings, Personalities of Language. *London: Gollancz, 1967.*

‡Le Grand-père et ses quatre petits fils. *Boston: Hickling, Swan and Brown, 1855. Compare Graze Pussy, New York City.*

Madame Fouqueau de Pussy, Authoress

MRS. FRIENDLY LEY*
  Mission Hills, California

BARONESS GABY VON BAGGE OF BOO
  (*New York Times*)

GASTON J. FEEBLEBUNNY
  U. S. A.

GEORGE BARETITS
  U. S. Army

GISELLA WERBERSERCH-PIFFEL†
  Actress
  Hollywood, California

*On whose career of amiability the curtain descended when
her husband's revolver, which he was cleaning in the kitchen,
went off.

†Perennial victim of prewar Hollywood jokers who liked to
telephone from poolside to ask if she was the Gisella
Werberserch-Piffel they had met in (e.g.) Monte Carlo the
previous summer; on receiving assurance to the contrary they
would pronounce grandly, "Ah! Then that must have been
another *Gisella Werberserch-Piffel!*" Compare Josette Legg
Snowball (*Actress, D'Oyly Carte Company*).

Mrs Friendly Ley, Mission Hills, California

HEINRICH LXXIV

Prince Heinrich the Seventy-Fourth of Reuss,
Thuringia, Germany

GRECIAN T. SNOOZE*
  Australian University Student (Class of 1950)

GROANER DIGGER†
  Undertaker
  Houston, Texas
  (*Today's Health*)

HALLOWEEN BUGGAGE
  The Charity Hospital
  New Orleans, Louisiana

PRINCE HEINRICH THE 74TH OF REUSS‡
  Jankendorf, Germany

HORACINE CLUTCH
  Pelham, New York

---

*Dunkling, op. cit.

†*Compare Goody P. Creep, Undertaker. The Quick-Park Funeral Home may be found at 617 Columbus Avenue, Sandusky.*

‡*Born 1798. Since 1693 all males in this ancient family have been named Heinrich.*

(Miss) Horsey de Horsey*
    Intimate friend of Lord Cardigan†

Hrothgar J. Habakkuk
    Vice-Chancellor, Oxford University
    Oxford, England

Hugh Pugh
    Landscape Architect
    London, England

Humperdink Fangboner‡
    Lumber Dealer, and
    Fanny Fangboner
    Nurse
    Sandusky, Ohio

I. C. Shivers
    Iceman
    (*John Hancock Life Insurance Company*)

Compare The Honorable Outerbridge Horsey, U.S. Ambassador to Czechoslovakia.

†*Who on a notable occasion banged on her door shouting, "My dearest, she's dead!"—referring to her late Ladyship, "Let' get married at once!"*

‡*Folks in Sandusky, as in some towns in Oklahoma seem to feel better having odd names. Other citizens of the area include Ovid Futch, Xenophon Hassenpflug, Kitty Ditty, and (from the Sandusky Register) E. Kickapoo Banfill, Lecturer.*

Miss Horsey de Horsey

IMA HOGG
  Social Leader
  Houston, Texas

IONA VICTORY BOND
  Victoria, British Columbia

I. O. SILVER
  (*Philadelphia Evening Bulletin*)

I. P. FRILLI*
  Master Mechanic
  Florence, Italy

IRIS FAIRCLOTH BLITCH
  Congresswoman
  Washington, D. C.

JOHN SENIOR, JUNIOR†
  New York City

Compare P. P. Fast, Fla., Mrs. Tiney Sprinkle, New York City, and Tom Passwater, Art Instruction School, Minneapolis, Minn. A Mr. Uren changed his name to Wren (1897)—understandably.

†*Who must bear partial responsibility for that deplorable nuisance, New York Airways.*

JOY BANG
   Actress
   New York City

JULY AUGUST SEPTEMBER
   (*Today's Health*)

JUSTIN TUNE
   Chorister
   Westminster Choir College (Class of 1947)
   Princeton, New Jersey

KATZ MEOW
   Hoquiam, Washington
   (*Collier's*)

KATZ PAJAMA COMPANY*
   New York City

Compare Climax Underwear Co., Cincinnati, O.

Katz Meow, Hoquiam, Washington

LARRY DERRYBERRY*
    Attorney General
    Oklahoma City, Oklahoma

LAVENDER SIDEBOTTOM†
    Masseuse, Elizabeth Arden
    New York City

LAWLESS & LYNCH
    Attorneys
    Jamaica, New York

LETTICE GOEDEBED
    Johannesburg, South Africa

LINUS KLUEMPER‡
    Jasper, Indiana

---

*Also Harry Derryberry, Lima, O., and Jerry Derryberry, Chattanooga, Tenn.

†N. b.: Epitaph of Mr. Longbottom, who died young: Arse longa, vita brevis.

‡Attained celebrity in August 1955 when a fan in his bedroom window wriggled five feet toward him and chopped off the big toe of his right foot.

LOUIS GEORGE MAURICE ADOLPH
ROCH ALBERT ABEL ANTONIO
ALEXANDRE NOÉ JEAN LUCIEN
DANIEL EUGENE JOSEPH-LE-BRUN
JOSEPHE-BARÊME THOMAS THOMAS-THC
PIERRE-CERBON PIERRE-MAUREL
BARTHELEMI ARTUS ALPHONSE BERTRAND
DIEUDONNE EMANUEL JOSUE VINCENT
LUC MICHEL JULES-DE-LA-PLANE JULES-
BAZIN JULIO-CESAR JULLIEN*
        Orchestra Conductor
        France

LOYAL LODGE NO. 296 KNIGHTS OF
PYTHIAS PONCA CITY OKLAHOMA SMITH†
        Ponca City, Oklahoma

LUSCIOUS PEA
        The Charity Hospital
        New Orleans, Louisiana

*Born in 1812, the Maestro was for obvious reasons known simply as The Conductor Jullien.

†Born August 21, 1876. Mencken, op. cit.

Lyulph Ydwallo Odin Nestor Egbert
Lyonel Toedmag Hugh Erchenwyne
Saxon Esa Cromwell Orma Nevill
Dysart Plantagenet Tollemache-
Tollemache
    Bentleigh, Otumoetai,
    Tauranga, New Zealand
    (*Burke's Peerage and Baronetage*)

Madonna Ghostly
    Teacher
    Washington, D. C.

Mrs. Maginis Oyster
    Social Leader
    San Raphael, California
    (*Social Register*)

Major Minor
    U. S. Army

Mark Clark Van Ark
    Toledo, Ohio

Mary Maloof Teabaggy, Boston

MARY LOUISE PANTZAROFF*
   Huron County, Ohio

MELISSY DALCINY CALDONY YANKEE
PANKEE DEVIL-TAKE-THE-IRISHMAN GARRISON
   Tryon City, North Carolina

(MISS) MEMORY LANE
   Roslyn High School, New York

MENE MENE TEKEL UPHARSIN POND
   Hartford, Connecticut

MERCY BUMPUS†
   Wife of "General Tom Thumb"

MOO, BOO, GOO, and LITTLE MISS MAY
   New Orleans, Louisiana

MOON UNIT ZAPPA and DWEEZLE ZAPPA
   Hollywood, California

*Compare Mary Maloof Teabaggy, Boston, Mass.

†Enjoyed the specialized distinction of being fought over by
the General and his tiny rival, Commodore Nutt.

MUSTAFA KUNT*
   Turkish Military Attaché
   Moscow, U. S. S. R.

NEWTON HOOTON
   Cambridge, Massachusetts

N. GUPPY†
   The Pond, Haddenham
   Cambridge, England

NITA BATH
   (*Philadelphia Evening Bulletin*)

NOBLE TEAT‡
   Still Pond, Maryland

Occasion of much ribald official cable traffic, along with his vis-à-vis, Major R. Rectanus, U.S. Assistant Military Attaché, Moscow. Of Gen. Plastiras (Greece) Winston Churchill expressed the hope that he did not have "feet of clay."

†*The fish is named for the family, not vice versa.*

‡*Compare Faithful Teate, Dublin "who wrote a quaint poem on the Trinity." (Encyclopedia Britannica)*

Norman Icenoggle
   (*Associated Press*)

Odile, Odelia, Olive, Oliver,
Olivia, Ophelia, Odelin, Octave,
Octavia, Ovide, Onesia, Olite, Otto,
Ormes, and Opta Maynard*
   Abbeville, Louisiana

O. Hell
   Contractor
   Alto Adige, Italy

Ophelia Legg
   Norwalk, Ohio

Orange Marmalade Lemon
   Wichita, Kansas

Original Bug
   Liverpool, England
   (*Liverpool Echo*)

*Dunkling, op. cit.

Original Bug, Liverpool

Osborn Outhouse
    Boston, Massachusetts

Peninnah Swingle Hogencamp Umbach
    Spiritualist Minister
    Charleston, South Carolina

Miss Pensive Cocke*
    Secretary
    U. S. Army Air Corps

Miss Pinkey Dickey Dukes
    Branchville, South Carolina

*Compare Mrs. Seeman Glasscock; J. Badcock, Editor,
London; B. Growcock, Teacher, Washington, D. C.; D.
Grewcock, Stockbroker, N. Y.; and the Griesedieck (beer)
family of St. Louis. The Koch Erecting Company is a major
supplier to New York City, while the Dicke Tool Company
operates in Bronxville, N. Y. Cinderella Hardcock and D.
Biggerdick studied with the Art Instruction School,
Minneapolis. Respectful attention is bestowed on the good
Cornish family of Trebilcock and concerned awareness on
Prof. A. O. J. Cockshut. W. J. Uglow Woolcock appears in
Boyle's Court Guide for 1915. Cf. P. H. Reaney, The Origin
of English Surnames. London: Routledge and Kegan Paul,
1967, p. 209 et seq.

PLATO FOUFAS
    Real Estate
    Chicago, Illinois

PLUMMER & LEEK
    Plumbers
    Sheringham, Norfolk
    (*London Times*)

POSITIVE WASERMANN JOHNSON*
    Evanston, Illinois

PRESERVED FISH, JR.†
    New Bedford, Massachusetts

PRIMROSE GOO
    Hawaii

RAPID INTEGRATION
    (*Newsweek*)

*"*Probably represents the indelicate humor of a medical
student.*"—H. L. Mencken,* The American Language,
Fourth Edition, New York: Alfred A. Knopf, 1936.

†*Born in 1766; partner in firm said to market whale oil in
two grades: "good and bad." His father and other forebears
bore the same name. "There is no foundation to the oft repeated
story that his name was bestowed by a New Bedford fisherman
who found him as an infant adrift at sea in an open boat."*
(Dictionary of American Biography)

Preserved Fish, Jr.

RONALD SUPENA
    Lawyer
    (*Philadelphia Evening Bulletin*)

ROSEBUD ROSENBLOOM
    Ethical Culture School
    New York City

ROSETTA STONE
    New York City

SALOME CASANOVA
    Havana, Cuba and Madrid, Spain

SANTIAGO NUDELMAN
    Publisher
    Brazil

MRS. SCREECH
    Singing Teacher
    Victoria, British Columbia

SHANDA LEAR*
    Battle Creek, Michigan

Of the Lear Jet Lears.

SHINE SOON SUN*
    Geophysicist
    Houston, Texas

SIDDHARTHA GREENBLATT
    (*Harper's Magazine*)

SILENCE BELLOWS†
    Editor
    (*Christian Science Monitor*)

SODAWATER BOTTLEWALLA
    Bombay, India
    (*New York Times*)

STRANGEWAYS PIGG STRANGEWAYS
    Cricket Star
    London, England

SUPARPORN POOPATTANA
    New York City

*Compare Moon Bong Kang, Korean Ambassador to Switzerland.

†Vermont Connecticut Royster is editor of the other reliable American paper, the Wall Street Journal.

Lt. Gen. H.H. Shri Shri Shri (etc... 108 times) Maharajadhiraj, the Maharega of Patiala

Lt. Gen. His Highness Shri Shri Shri
Shri Shri Shri Shri Shri Shri Shri
Shri Shri Shri Shri Shri Shri Shri
Shri Shri Shri Shri Shri Shri Shri
Shri Shri Shri Shri Shri Shri Shri
Shri Shri Shri Shri Shri Shri Shri
Shri Shri Shri Shri Shri Shri Shri
Shri Shri Shri Shri Shri Shri Shri
Shri Shri Shri Shri Shri Shri Shri
Shri Shri Shri Shri Shri Shri Shri
Shri Shri Shri Shri Shri Shri Shri
Shri Shri Shri Shri Shri Shri Shri
Shri Shri Shri Shri Shri Shri Shri
Shri Shri Shri Shri Shri Shri Shri
Shri Shri Shri Shri Shri Shri Shri
Shri Shri Shri Shri Shri Shri Shri
Maharajadhiraj Raj Rajeshwar
Shri Maharja-i-Rajgan Mararaja
Sir Yadvindra Singh Mahendra
Bahadur, Yadu Vanshavatans Bhatti
Kul Bhushan Rajpramukh of Patiala*
India and London, England

*Born in 1913, the Maharaja of Patiala is also the leader of
the Sikh community, all of whose members bear the surname
Singh (meaning lion). The sequence in the first part of the
title is usually contracted to "Shri 108."

SUPPLY CLAPP THWING
    Harvard College (Class of 1837)

MRS. TACKABERRY MCADOO
    Social Leader
    New York City
    (*Social Register*)

TETLEY IRONSIDES TETLEY JONES
    Chairman, Tetley Tea Company
    London, England

T. HEE
    Restaurant Employee
    New York City

THUSNELDA NEUSBICKLE
    Wellesley College
    Wellesley, Massachusetts

TRAILING ARBUTUS VINES*
    Cumberland Mountains, Tennessee

UFUK RESTAURANT
    Izmir, Turkey

Mencken, op. cit.

Ufuk Restaurant, Izmir, Turkey

UNABLE TO FORNICATE*
   Indian Chief
   Northwestern U. S.

MRS. V. D. WHYNOT†
   U. S. A.

MR. VENUS BONAPARTE
   (*London Times*)

VERBAL FUNDERBURK
   Lakeland, Florida

MR. VICE‡
   Malefactor
   New Orleans, Louisiana

VIRGINIA MAY SWEATT STRONG
   Memphis, Tennessee

Reported by Mencken. Fly-Fornication was a good Puritan name.

†*Linda Whynot was convicted of lewd and wanton behavior in the Gemini Hotel, Providence, R. I.* (Providence Journal)

‡*Arrested 890 times and convicted 421, probably a record.* (International Herald Tribune)

Mr. Vice, Malefactor, New Orleans

VIOLET ORGAN*
    Art Historian
    New York City

VOLUME DINGLE†
    Tampa, Florida

MR. VROOM‡
    Motorcycle Dealer
    Port Elizabeth, South Africa
    (*New York Times*)

WARREN PEACE
    Williams College, Massachusetts

SIR W. C. DAMPIER-WHETHAM
    Upwater Lodge, Cambridge

WELCOME BABY DARLING
    Greenwich, Connecticut

Biographer of the American painter Robert Henri. She never married. Compare Violet Butt, Washington, D.C., and Noble Butt, Boston.

†*His wife threw out his pants, containing his life's savings.* (Tampa Tribune)

‡*Compare Joy Auto Collision, Toronto, and Fuzle-Rub Motor Training School, Calcutta.*

Mr Vroom, Motorcycle Dealer, Port Elizabeth, South Africa

WILLIAM McKINLEY LOUISIANA
LEVEEBUST SMITH*
  Richmond, Virginia

WYRE & TAPPING†
  Detectives
  New York City

YELBERTSON ABRAHAM TITTLE
  Quarterback, New York Giants
  New York City

ZEZOZOSE ZADFRACK‡
  California

ZODA VIOLA KLONTZ GAZOLA
  U. S. A.

DR. ZOLTAN OVARY
  Gynecologist, New York Hospital
  New York City

*Mencken, op. cit.

†The Office of Nomenclature Stabilization has a photograph
of this establishment.

‡Natural son of C. Manson, Mass Murderer, by a Miss
Atkins.

INDEX OF FAMILY NAMES